Awesome African Animals!

Giraffes Are Awesome!

by Lisa J. Amstutz

Consultant: Jackie Gai, DVM
Exotic Animal Veterinarian
Vacaville, California

CAPSTONE PRESS
a capstone imprint

A+ Books are published by Capstone Press,
1710 Roe Crest Drive, North Mankato, Minnesota 56003
www.capstonepub.com

Library of Congress Cataloging-in-Publication Data
Amstutz, Lisa J., author.
  Giraffes are awesome! / by Lisa J. Amstutz.
      pages cm. — (A+ books. Awesome African animals)
  Summary: "Describes the characteristics, habitat, behavior, life cycle, and threats to giraffes living in the wild
of Africa"—Provided by publisher.
  Audience: Ages 5–8.
  Audience: K to grade 3.
  Includes bibliographical references and index.
  ISBN 978-1-4914-1761-4 (library binding)
  ISBN 978-1-4914-1767-6 (paperback)
  ISBN 978-1-4914-1773-7 (eBook PDF)
1. Giraffe—Juvenile literature. 2. Animals—Africa—Juvenile literature. I. Title.

  QL737.U56A534 2015
  599.638—dc23   2014023670

Editorial Credits
Erika Shores and Mari Bolte, editors; Cynthia Della-Rovere, designer; Svetlana Zhurkin, media researcher;
Morgan Walters, production specialist

Photo Credits
Newscom: Photoshot/NHPA/Daryl Balfour, 24; Shutterstock: Achim Baque, 23, Black Sheep Media (grass),
throughout, BlueRingMedia, 8 (right), Christian Musat, cover (bottom), 32, Coffeemill, cover (top left), 4 (left),
15 (right), Dennis Donohue, 6—7, Dmitry Pichugin, 26—27, fishandfish, 6 (left) and throughout (background),
irakite, 12, jaroslava V, cover (right), 1, Jeff Grabert, 19, Jo Crebbin, 21, Joe McDonald, 18, Kletr, back cover (top),
26 (top), lewald, 9, Marci Paravia, 13, MattiaATH, 20, Mogens Trolle, 11, Mohamed Zain, 15 (left), moizhusein,
29, mythja, 10 (top right), Nadezhda Bolotina, 22, orxy, 25, Pal Teravagimov, 28, Pyty, 4—5, Shinga, 17, spirit of
America (African landscape), back cover and throughout, stieberszabolcs, 4 (middle), studio online, 14, Tzido
Sun, 8 (left), Vaclav Volrab, 10 (left, bottom)

Note to Parents, Teachers, and Librarians
This Awesome African Animals book uses full color photographs and a nonfiction format to
introduce the concept of giraffes. *Giraffes Are Awesome!* is designed to be read aloud to a pre-reader
or to be read independently by an early reader. Photographs help listeners and early readers
understand the text and concepts discussed. The book encourages further learning by including
the following sections: Table of Contents, Glossary, Read More, Internet Sites, and Index. Early
readers may need assistance using these features.

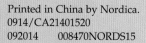
Printed in China by Nordica.
0914/CA21401520
092014   008470NORDS15

Table of Contents

All About Giraffes

Stretch! A giraffe reaches high in a tree. It nibbles a tasty leaf. Giraffes are the tallest animals on earth. They grow up to 18 feet (5.5 meters) tall.

Spots cover a giraffe's body. No two patterns are the same. The spots hide them from predators. Giraffes match the trees that dot the grassy savanna in Africa.

Africa

Where Giraffes Live

A giraffe's neck is as long as its legs. Short hair, called a mane, grows down the back. Inside the neck are seven bones. Your neck has seven bones too. They are much smaller than a giraffe's though!

A giraffee's long neck makes it hard to jump up quickly when lying down. So giraffes often nap standing up.

The bumps on a giraffe's head are called ossicones. They are made of bone, and are covered with skin and hair. Males, or bulls, use them to fight each other. They crash their heads and necks together.
They fight over females, called cows.

Dinner Time

Giraffes are herbivores. That means they eat only plants. It takes lots of food to fill a giraffe's stomach. It may eat 75 pounds (34 kilograms) of food in one day. A giraffe eats in the morning and evening. It rests in the heat of the day and at night.

Giraffes eat leaves, twigs, and small branches. They grab food from the tops of trees with their long tongues. A giraffe's tongue is as long as your arm!

Giraffes love eating from acacia trees. The tree has sharp thorns. But the giraffe's tongue and gums are tough. Its strong teeth crush the thorns. Thick saliva protects its mouth.

A giraffe's stomach has four parts. The food goes into the first part. Then the animal burps it up and chews it some more. Now it is called cud. After a while, the giraffe swallows the cud. It then passes through the rest of the giraffe's stomach.

Family Ties

After age 5, a female giraffe can have a calf. A newborn calf is 6 feet (1.8 m) tall. It starts walking soon after birth. The calf drinks its mother's milk at first. Later it will learn to eat leaves.

For its first week, a calf hides in tall grass. Its mother stays nearby. Then it joins other calves in the herd. Their mothers take turns watching them. Living in a herd keeps calves safe. Once grown, giraffes in the wild can live to 25 years old.

Danger Lurks

A giraffe can drink 10 gallons (38 liters) of water at a time. It may go days without drinking. When it drinks, the giraffe spreads its legs and bends down. During this time, predators can attack.

Giraffes go to watering holes in groups. They take turns watching for predators. They warn the others with grunts and snorts when danger is near.

Adult giraffes are too big for most predators to kill. But they have to watch out for lions and crocodiles. Hyenas and cheetahs can kill calves.

Giraffes have good eyesight and hearing. Their height lets them spot predators far away. So zebras and other animals like to graze near them.

25

When a predator comes near, giraffes run away. They can run up to 35 miles (56 kilometers) per hour for short distances. They can kick hard too. A powerful kick can kill a lion.

Saving Giraffes

Humans are the biggest danger to giraffes. People hunt them for their meat and skins. Farmers cut down the trees giraffes eat to grow crops and raise livestock.

Today most giraffes live in parks and reserves. There they are safe from hunters. People plant trees for them. If we protect giraffes, these awesome giants will always roam Africa.

Glossary

cud (KUHD)—half-eaten food that an animal burps up and chews again

graze (GRAYZ)—to eat grass and other plants

herbivore (UR-buh-vor)—an animal that eats only plants

herd (HURD)—a large group of animals that lives or moves together

mane (MAYN)—long, thick hair that grows on the head and neck of some animals like lions and horses

ossicone (OS-uh-kohn)—a hornlike bump on a giraffe's head

predator (PRED-uh-tur)—an animal that hunts other animals for food

reserve (ri-ZURV)—an area of land set aside by the government for a special purpose, such as protecting plants and animals

saliva (suh-LYE-vuh)—the clear liquid in the mouth

savanna (suh-VAN-uh)—a flat, grassy area of land with few or no trees

Read More

Murray, Julie. *Giraffes*. African Animals. Minneapolis: ABDO Publishing Company, 2012.

Raatma, Lucia. *Giraffes*. Nature's Children. New York: Children's Press, 2014.

Shea, Mary Molly. *Giraffes*. Animals That Live in the Grasslands. New York: Gareth Stevens Publishing, 2011.

Internet Sites

FactHound offers a safe, fun way to find Internet sites related to this book. All of the sites on FactHound have been researched by our staff.

Here's all you do:
Visit *www.facthound.com*
Type in this code: 9781491471614

Super-cool stuff! Check out projects, games and lots more at **www.capstonekids.com**

Critical Thinking Using the Common Core

1. Why might a giraffe's long neck make it difficult to get up quickly? (Key Ideas and Details)

2. Describe how a giraffe's tongue helps it eat. (Integration of Knowledge and Ideas)

3. The text on page 10 says male giraffes use their ossicones for fighting. What do you think females use their ossicones for? (Key Ideas and Details)

Index